With These Words

A prayerbook of gratitude

ISBN: 979-8-218-71473-4

Cover Design by Lydia Lavi Triplett

Publisher: With A Whisper

Printed in the USA

A special thank you to my supportive family and friends, who are on this earth and beyond, and to those who find solace in the prayers and gratitude enclosed in this book.

--- Table of Contents ---

--- A Personal Story ---

A dear friend who was going through challenges in life once asked me if I prayed. "Of course, I pray every morning," I replied. I didn't think much of the question until they asked if I could teach them how to pray. At that moment, I stood dumbstruck, not because of the initial question, but because of the latter. I did not know how to teach someone how to pray.

I had been saying prayers since I was young, and my faith, which I challenged at every opportunity, was part of my upbringing. However, I replied, "Absolutely, I can do that." In humor, I explained that I was not savvy enough to teach prayers, but I could recite what I say every morning, and they could write down what resonated with them.

For the next hour, my friend and I strived to make good use of that precious moment, praying, writing, clarifying, but time got the best of us, and we pledged to revisit our mission later. Within weeks, life's challenges overtook my dear friend, and they consciously chose to leave this earthly journey and reside with God.

My dear friend and I never had the chance to revisit our mission or continue exploring how prayer, gratitude, and love could have helped overcome the challenges of our life experiences. Although time will not allow us to revisit that moment, what inspired me most is that my dear friend dared to reach out and inquire about prayer. This alone meant the world to me because it showed me that being open to prayer gave a sense of grounding. Even in its smallest increment, the ability to share prayer, gratitude, and love with my dear friend allowed us to experience a connection that will reside in my heart forever.

--- Preface ---

We come into this world with everything we need from the start, where God, Source, Spirit, Allah, or however you choose to refer to the all-knowing presence, has always provided us with the capability to practice the art of gratitude. Still, over time, we have forgotten how to apply it.

Sometimes, life seems to require too much from us, and at times may even appear too much to bear. However, the obstacles we face in our lifetime may not be meant to defeat us, but to provide us with tools to teach us how to rise above them and look at them from a different perspective. We have a choice to let life's challenges consume us, or we can take a step back and look at those challenges from a position of love and gratitude, allowing us to find the link or lesson within to overcome them.

As we evolve, we learn that we are interconnected in more ways than we can imagine. We begin to understand that our vitality can serve us better when our frequency is high and we attach to positive energy. Nevertheless, we persist in detaching from our centers, searching and connecting to people and things we assume will make us happy, allowing these things to pull us into a web of undesirable patterns, lowering our frequency. Perhaps a good way to return to our center and to move toward a higher frequency is to practice the art of gratitude by simply observing life's challenges from a different perspective.

The purpose of this book is to universally raise our vibrational frequency through simple gratitude and open our eyes to those precious moments that are always within reach. To appreciate the little things we take for granted every day, and the gifts we inherit when we enter this world but detach from when we strive for more or feel that more is required of us.

If we raise our Consciousness, we may be able to change our perception of the world and gain a deeper understanding of ourselves.

This book may not resonate with everyone, but it is open to anyone who chooses to put themselves in a place of being receptive to transformation, to find what grounds them, and follow that path, enlightening them to a greater understanding of self and their surroundings.

Happiness is all around us if we step into its vibrational frequency, and this book is merely an additional tool for your spiritual toolbox to assist in recognizing gratitude in a different light.

Have gratitude for the now, open your heart, and listen. This is your journey, experience it.

--- Recommendation ---

The prayers, gratitude, healing mantras, and meditation, within the framework, are written to be spoken daily, however, they are not required to be done daily to be effective. It is more important that you are present when the words are spoken than when they are spoken without you being present.

The context of the Prayers and Gratitude pages is written in plural vs. singular so that a shared narrative can be realized. The repetition of text throughout the pages is deliberate, to work towards developing an intention of appreciation, transformation, and growth, raising our conscious awareness in a collective effort to connect to something larger than oneself.

x

If a page does not resonate with you, put it aside. If you need to verbally add to the text so it makes more sense to you, add it. Bringing in positive energy and raising your vibration is the objective. Some find it helpful to play soothing music during prayer and meditation. However, in time and with practice, you may find that music is no longer necessary, but the rhythmic sound of your breath will be.

--- Why Protect Your Sanctuary? ---

When you step through the pages of this book, it is important to protect the surroundings of your sanctuary, as you will be an open source of energy. Remove yourself from distraction, set your intentions with positivity and light, quiet your mind, and allow yourself to be present.

With These Words

A prayerbook of gratitude

-- Sanctuary Protection Prayer --

With these words, I ask God to protect the surroundings of my sanctuary, letting no negative energy, no negative entities, no evil spirits, and no bad karma penetrate this space or the occupants inside, letting in only light, love, and generosity.

--- Prayers and Gratitude---

With these words, we humbly pray, and thank you, God, for hearing our prayers.

God, thank you for keeping us, our families, and our loved ones safe from harm and danger.

God, thank you for providing us with food, shelter, and clothing, and thank you, God, for forgiving us for our sins.

3

God, thank you for the courage and strength you give us to get out of bed every day, and walk this earth to try to understand our life's purpose.

Thank you for the clarity and wisdom you have given us to understand our journey, our path, and how to discern.

God, thank you for sending the essence of your presence to this earth to reunite our vibrational frequency, enhance our Consciousness, and provide a pathway of light for us to follow your truth, believe in your guidance, and live by love to get back home.

5

God, thank you for forgiving us for our sins of past and present, for opening the hearts of those we have sinned against allowing them to forgive us, and for opening our hearts, allowing us to forgive those who have sinned against us, giving us all a clean slate, a fresh start, and freedom of choice for any incarnation here.

God, thank you for removing from our hearts any anger, bitterness, hate, resentment, jealousy, and fear, and replacing these with love, kindness, compassion, sympathy, and empathy, allowing us to feel love, receive love, and give love more abundantly.

God, thank you for raising our vibrational frequency so we can connect with those who carry similar frequencies and higher, but not to neglect those of lower frequency, as they may need our help.

God, thank you for opening our souls so that we may learn the values of the lessons you have given us, so that when our time comes, our transitions are smooth, and our journeys are safe.

God, thank you for providing us with the hosted bodies we rely on every day to navigate this world, and for the awareness to treat them properly.

Thank you for our ability to connect with the earth and nature, and for syncing our hearts to the vibrational frequency of the universe.

God, we thank you for the beautiful souls, who have been so kind as to offer a hand to pull us up when we need help, a shoulder for us to lean on, an ear to listen to our plight, or those just willing to hold the light when we can't find our way.

God, thank you for these beautiful souls, and we pray that you bestow on them all the unconditional love, light, and generosity available to them.

God, thank you for the support of our families, our higher minds, our guides, our guardians, and our Angels.

Thank you, God, for our extended families, our friends, our neighbors, our acquaintances, and all the souls we connect with daily.

God, thank you for the abundance of wealth you have provided all of us, emotionally, spiritually, physically, and mentally. An abundance of wealth so that we are never in need, never in debt, and never without, for any incarnation here.

God, thank you for listening to our wills, with their best intentions, to be heard throughout the heavens and honored by the universe.

God, thank you for this amazing journey as an eternal being living a human experience, a journey that has allowed us to open our eyes, our hearts, and be present, a journey that permits us to bring unconditional love into our hearts and share it with the world on your behalf.

God, we are thankful that you continue to guide us in our walk of life and carry us when we can walk no longer.

God, we are grateful for your blessing of our prayers and gratitude and pray that you bestow on us all the unconditional love, light, and generosity available to us.

With these words, we pray.
In the name of the Holy Spirit,
Amen.

--- Healing Mantras ---

God, thank you for the healing of this home. Its exterior, its upper limits, its lower limits, its space in between.

God, thank you for the healing of this home so that no negative energy, no negative entities, no evil spirits, and no bad karma can penetrate this home or the occupants inside.

God, thank you for the healing of this foundation. The foundation upon which our home sits and on which we stand while in our home.

God, thank you for the healing of this foundation so that no negative energy, no negative entities, no evil spirits, and no bad karma can penetrate this foundation.

17

God, thank you for the healing of the stone. The stone that paves the driveways, the stone that creates the walkways, and the patio floors, the stone that secures the retaining walls and shapes the stairwells, the stone that graces our lands.

God, thank you for the healing of the stone so that no negative energy, no negative entities, no evil spirits, and no bad karma can penetrate the stone.

God, thank you for the healing of the trees. The trees that have rooted themselves so strongly into the ground. The trees that have risen so tall to reach the heavens.

God, thank you for the healing of the trees so that no negative energy, no negative entities, no evil spirits, and no bad karma can penetrate the trees.

19

God, thank you for the healing of the Earth. The Earth on which we place our feet to absorb its energy, the Earth from which you have pulled us to create us and set us to bring us home. The Earth from which Mother Gaia has offered her beauty, her love, and her light.

God, thank you for the healing of the Earth so that no negative energy, no negative entities, no evil spirits, and no bad karma can penetrate the Earth.

God, thank you for the healing of the air. The air in which we breathe. The air through which our light passes. The air in which our energy flows from one to another.

God, thank you for the healing of the air so that no negative energy, no negative entities, no evil spirits, and no bad karma can penetrate the air.

God, thank you for the healing of the water. The water that falls from the sky. The water that fills our body. The water that flows through our yards, our cities, our countries, our continents, and our oceans. The water, with its commitment to nourish and to heal, not to damage and destroy.

God, thank you for the healing of the water, so that no negative energy, no negative entities, no evil spirits, and no bad karma can penetrate the water.

God, thank you for the healing of the fire. The fire that burns in our hearts, the fire that heats our homes, cooks our food, and eradicates our lands. The fire, with its commitment to nourish and to heal, not to damage and destroy.

God, thank you for the healing of the fire, so that no negative energy, no negative entities, no evil spirits, and no bad karma can penetrate the fire.

God, thank you for the healing of us living creatures we call eternal beings sharing a human experience, the healing of us living creatures we call animals and plants, and the healing of us living creatures from other galaxies and entities that have come to this Earth, offering their kindness, love, and generosity, and assisting in raising our vibrational frequencies.

God, thank you for the healing of us living creatures so that no negative energy, no negative entities, no evil spirits, and no bad karma can penetrate us living creatures.

God, thank you for the healing of these beautiful souls we call our higher minds, our families, our children, our grandchildren, our great-grandchildren, our friends, our neighbors, and the souls we connect with daily.

God, thank you for the healing of these beautiful souls so that no negative energy, no negative entities, no evil spirits, and no bad karma can penetrate these beautiful souls.

God, thank you for opening our hearts
to be filled with gratitude so that we can
feel love, give love, and receive love.

Thank you for guiding our souls in
learning the lessons you have intended
for us to learn, so that when our time
comes, our transitions are smooth, and
our journeys are safe.

God, thank you for our wills, with their best intentions, that they are heard throughout the earth, the universe, and the heavens, and honored.

With these words, we humbly pray. Thank you, God, for hearing our mantras.

-- Meditation Protection Prayer --

God, thank you for allowing me to call upon the Archangels.

I call upon Archangel Michael (South),

I call upon Archangel Gabriel (West),

I call upon Archangel Raphael (East), and

I call upon Archangel Uriel (North).

I call upon this team of Archangels with their flaming sword of truth to pierce through the center of this sanctuary and protect it with their love and light.

I call upon this team of Archangels to protect all boundaries of this property, all spaces of its interior, and the upper and lower limits of the area within.

I call upon this team of Archangels to work with God, our guides, and our angels in keeping us safe, away from harm and danger, letting no negative energy, no negative entities, no evil spirits, and no bad karma penetrate these spaces or the occupants inside, letting in only light, love, and generosity.

--- Meditation ---

Take a few minutes to sit still. It's not necessary to sit for long periods or in any special seating style, which will come in time. Just find comfort, ask for clarity, breathe slowly, listen to the rhythm of your breath, and feel the energy of the breath flowing through your body.

All we have is now, not yesterday, and not tomorrow. It is more important to feel gratitude for the present moment than to harp on a moment that serves no purpose.

You are always where you are supposed to be. Trust your life.

--- Notes ---

32